Walk Through History on the *Freedom Trail*

by Wes Payton

HOUGHTON MIFFLIN BOSTON

The Birth of Boston

In 1630 a group of Puritans founded the Massachusetts Bay Colony. A colony is a region settled by emigrants but controlled by their parent country. Puritans were people who left Britain because they wanted the freedom to worship as they wished. John Winthrop led some of the Puritans to a new settlement. They called it Boston. In 1632 Boston became the capital of the Massachusetts Bay Colony.

Boston, Massachusetts in the mid-1600s

Colonists in Boston riot over British taxes.

The Call for Freedom

Boston grew quickly. By the mid-1700s, Boston was one of the largest and most important cities in the American colonies. The colonies wanted to be independent, or free, of British rule. People in Boston were some of the leaders in the fight. They were angry because the British taxed the colonists without giving them a voice in their government.

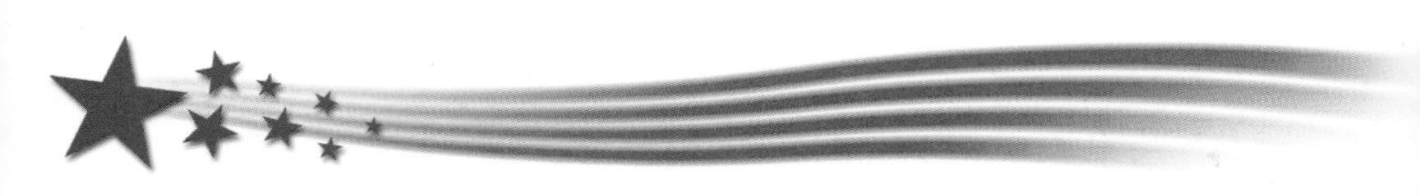

American soldiers in battle, 1775

Walking Through History

The colonies went to war with Britain. This war is called the American Revolution. The first battles of the American Revolution took place in and around Boston. Many of our country's founders and early heroes lived in Boston. You can see many important places from that time on the Freedom Trail. This is a three-mile route through the city. Let's walk on the Freedom Trail together.

The Freedom Trail, Boston

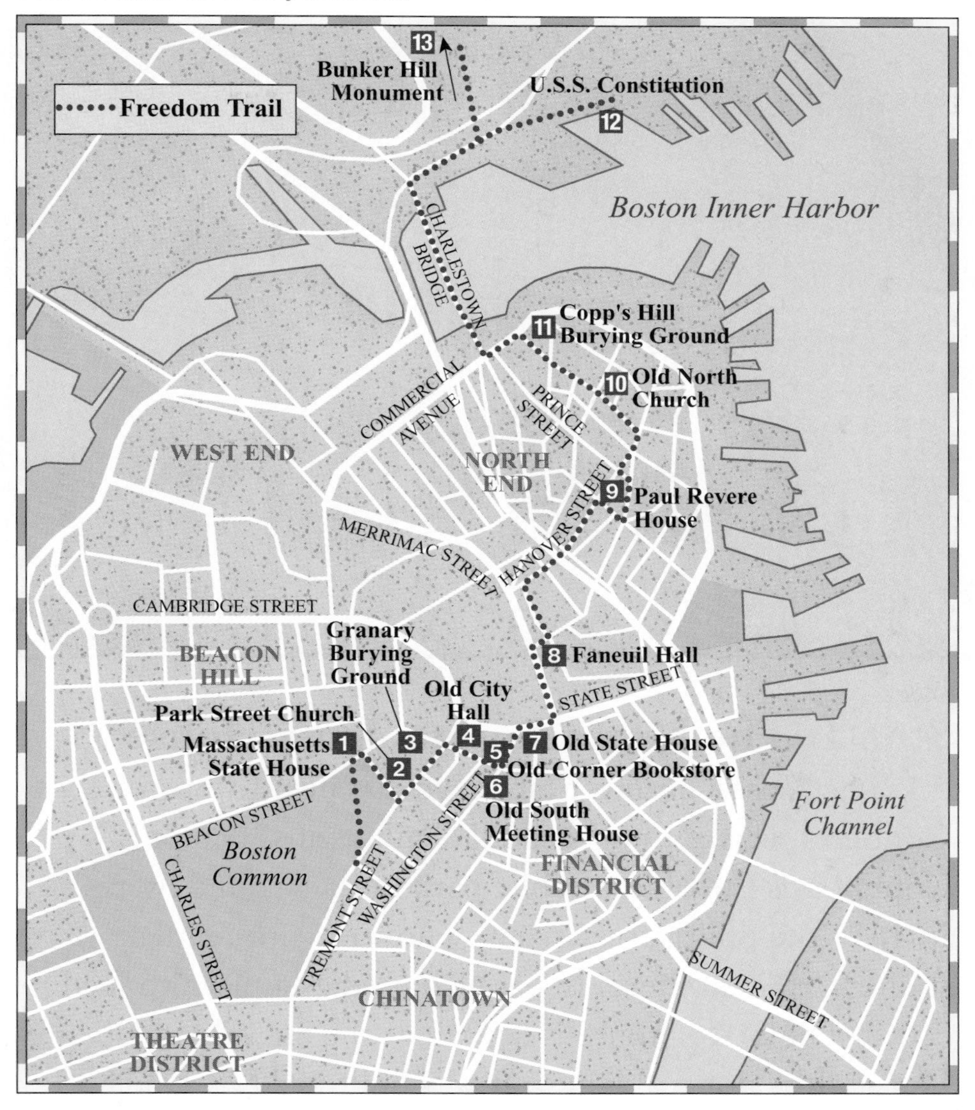

Stop 1: The Massachusetts State House

The Massachusetts State House is next to Boston Common, where the Freedom Trail begins. Boston Common is the oldest public park in the United States. In 1634 the militia, or citizens who were not regular soldiers, trained there. It was also used as a place to feed cattle. The State House is known as the "new" State House. It is not really new. It was built in 1798! Today, the government of Massachusetts still uses this building.

Stop 2: Park Street Church

Park Street Church was built in 1809. During the War of 1812, gunpowder was stored in the church's basement. The song "America" (also known as "My Country 'Tis of Thee") was first sung here on July 4, 1832. William Lloyd Garrison made his first speech against slavery in Park Street Church.

Stop 3: Granary Burying Ground

Many famous people are buried here. We can see the graves of such patriots as Paul Revere, John Hancock, and Samuel Adams. Nearby is King's Chapel. It was built in 1754. The first governor of the Massachusetts Bay Colony, John Winthrop, is buried in the cemetery by the chapel.

Stop 4: Old City Hall

Old City Hall is also the site, or location, of the first public school. Benjamin Franklin attended this school, called the Boston Latin School. He was born in Boston. Today, a statue of Franklin stands in front of Old City Hall. Franklin was an inventor, statesman, writer, and signer of the Declaration of Independence.

Stop 5: Old Corner Bookstore

The Old Corner Bookstore was built as an apothecary shop, or pharmacy. It was also an office and the home of Thomas Crease. In the 1800s, famous writers are believed to have met in this store. Among the writers were Nathaniel Hawthorne, Henry Wadsworth Longfellow, and Ralph Waldo Emerson. Today, the Boston Globe newspaper occupies the building, constructed in 1712.

Stop 6: Old South Meeting House

The Old South Meeting House was built as a Puritan church in 1729. Later, it became a place where colonists came to speak their minds. This is where the colonists met and debated on December 16, 1773, just before the Boston Tea Party.

Stop 7: The Old State House

The Old State House has been used in many ways. Built in 1713, it was first used by the British as their headquarters for Massachusetts Bay Colony. There is a circle of stones on the street outside. They show the site of the Boston Massacre. Here, British soldiers killed five patriots on March 5, 1770. After the revolution, it was the State House for Massachusetts. Today, the building is a museum.

Stop 8: Faneuil Hall

Peter Faneuil (FAN yehl) was a wealthy merchant. He built this hall in 1742 and used it as a public market and a meeting place. Today, it is still used for these purposes.

Stop 9: Paul Revere House

The Paul Revere House is the oldest building in downtown Boston. On April 18, 1775, Paul Revere left here to make his midnight ride to Lexington. He wanted to warn people that British troops were marching from Boston to Concord.

Stop 10: The Old North Church

Two lanterns were hung from the steeple of the Old North Church to signal the start of Paul Revere's midnight ride. The church was built in 1723.

Stop 11: Copp's Hill Burying Ground

The hill beneath this old graveyard is high, and you can see very far. Copp's Hill is where British troops fired their cannons during the Battle of Bunker Hill in 1775.

Stop 12: U.S.S. *Constitution, Old Ironsides*

The U.S.S. *Constitution* is the oldest ship in the United States Navy. Its nickname is *Old Ironsides*. In the War of 1812, shots fired from British ships bounced right off its sides. Built in 1797, the ship still sets sail today.

Stop 13: Bunker Hill Monument

Bunker Hill Monument marks the site where the first major battle of the American Revolution took place. On June 17, 1775, colonial forces battled British soldiers who occupied the city. Their bravery against the British encouraged the colonists to fight on.

This is our final stop on the Freedom Trail. Did you enjoy the tour?